# The Healing Pen

A promise to be kept...

Dr. Imroza Arman

BookLeaf Publishing

India | USA | UK

Made with ❤ on the BookLeaf Publishing Platform

www.bookleafpub.in

www.bookleafpub.com

# Dedication

*This book is dedicated to different instances that have happened to me, might be for a person for whom I picked up my pen.*
*This one's for you..*
*If you know what, and you probably know why..*


*You must trust me, I am telling a story :)*

# Preface

*"The Healing Pen" is more than a collection of poems — it is a journey of love, promises, and the quiet strength that hope gives us. Every word stitched into these pages carries the weight of a promise I once made to someone.*

*This book is dedicated to that one soul — the person who inspired me to believe in the power of healing, through love, through faith, and through the act of simply being present. I once promised him that I would write a book, and this — this is my heart keeping that promise. Each poem here is a whisper from the spaces between pain and peace, between longing and belonging. It is my humble attempt to capture the emotions that sometimes feel too vast for speech but find their home in poetry. Through this healing pen, I have bled, mended, and grown, and I hope that as you turn these pages, you too find pieces of your own healing journey mirrored within.*

*This book belongs to him. And it belongs to anyone who has ever loved so that they found themselves transformed. Enjoy the journey that took two years to conquer.*

*With gratitude and love,*

*Imroza*

# Acknowledgements

*Some journeys are meant to be walked quietly, with only the heart as a witness. "The Healing Pen" was born in silence, in moments unseen, written for someone who may never know the full depth of these words. This book exists because of a soul who unknowingly became the ink in my pen and the light in my darker hours. Every poem is a whispered letter, a quiet offering, a piece of a conversation that was never spoken aloud.*

*To those who have loved, lost, healed, and hoped — you will find yourself in these pages too. And to the one who inspired it all: you are everywhere in these lines, even if the world will never know.*

*Finally to the pen – thank you for being my companion at all.*


*With a heart full of quiet gratitude,*
*Imroza*

# 1. "The Moon"

*Where the world fades, standalone the moon pulls you*
*up till the terrace...*
*I walk the path where we once strayed,*
*In shadows where our laughter stayed.*
*Then you walk alone in the domain of the moonlight*
*Praising together about its sight..*
*The waves recite your gentle name,*
*A lullaby that sounds the same,*
*The moon started singing -*
*You & I are under the same night sky,*
*Every time you close your eyes you will see a*
*selenophile..*
*Every night you look up to the sky*
*The crests that the moon behold would feel shy..*
*The moon stared at you mysteriously;*
*With your eyes closed you would think of her & whisper*
*a word as if you are telling her story,*
*The stars and the galaxies would smile listening to your*
*words..*
*The stars look on with silent eyes,*
*Reflecting truths we once disguised,*
*Yet in this stillness, I can hear*
*Your voice like wind, forever near.*
*The moon, a witness from above,*

*Reminds my soul of endless love.*
*Beneath its glow, I see you there,*
*Your image in midnight air,*
*A moment caught in tender light,*
*A person who danced with me at midnight..*
*Since you are gone, the moon remains,*
*Still lighting up these midnight lanes,*
*Where memory and hope entwine,*
*And all that's lost begins to shine.*
*At that moment you would feel a peaceful breeze*
*trespassing your ears ,*
*Whispering slowly that the selenophile you remembered*
*is under the same sky thinking about how you might..*
*Smiling, wishing, blinking her sight...*
*and calling her 'the moon' on the verge of the night...*

# 2. "Silent Hope"

*Stubborn heart , some twisted games,*
*I wanted in silence that*
*was living for the maybe's & what if's...*
*But it wasn't mine & wasn't his,*
*Still making me feel*
*we belonged to each other in bliss.*
*Yet pushed you away when bewildered with the fear of*
*losing.*
*But how to erase a love not gone?*
*How could I let go & move on..?*
*At some point I thought love would conquer the pain...*
*And though the world had turned the page,*
*I stood frozen and lost in age,*
*Yet beneath the sorrow, beneath the ache,*
*A tiny flame refused to break.*
*A silent hope— I couldn't name,*
*Too shy to burn, too strong to tame.*
*It whispered, "Maybe he still cares,"*
*In lonely nights and silent prayers.*
*Muted volumes of unwavering love & support*
*throughout,*
*Indelibly marked my soul;*
*A testament to the immeasurable value he beholds in my*
*life,*

*His presence takes precedence over all else...*
*His smile of Radiance & Heart overflowing with joy*
*Would forever hold the title of the "Most Cherished!"*
*A memory that I'll relive countless times in the Chords*
*of the Guitar...*
*Still holding onto a small, childish Hope*
*that--*
*There's someone out there in this crazy wild world, so*
*completely & utterly meant for me...*
*that --*
*"Even the stars will sigh & gaze at us with relief at our*
*last meeting...!"*

# 3. "And all that happened.."

*And what all happened??*
*It gave her a heart but never gave her an opportunity to*
*seek love!*
*While she could write him over thousands of pages, she*
*could never write for her own self...*
*What else was there in the world except his eyes.*
*His audacity to heal her makes her feel better always;*
*His presence was only what mattered..*
*She always wished that if somehow fate would become*
*that insignificant,*
*All those might have, could have, should have turned out*
*to be true.. She wished!!*
*The right person at the wrong time has always made her*
*sad*
*& her grief has affected him too...*
*Sometimes she is broken enough to hold her emotions..*
*Trust those words which say that --*
*"The one who holds the childish behaviour, has got the*
*brilliant art of hiding the darkest pains.."*
*Thousands fell in love, but she couldn't even see in his*
*eyes..*
*Feelings were gutted within her ;*
*Stubborn to tell that she is a writer,*
*but never found those proper words to express her*

*thoughts..*

*Being anguished what destiny has always played*
*She confronts her Lord, why He made her pay such a*
*great debt,*
*that she couldn't even bear the weight.*
*Encroached him to make time for her but as if he was ok*
*with the distance...*
*Crazy she! Her affection blossomed furthermore itself*
*with the distance!*
*Someone close to her asked- what did it look like? why*
*did you fall for, why Him??*
*She replied - even though he hasn't left any remarks, yet*
*he is the one where her heart lies..*
*At the end of the day, Calming her down in peace,*
*Pacified her whenever she has broken down.*
*Thousands of men staring at her,*
*But she fell for the one whose eyes were towards the*
*ground...*
*When she closed her eyes she found him,*
*When she looked into his eyes she got to see herself*
*within...*
*If she dies, how long will she be remembered? That's*
*why maybe she talks about him for a while,*
*Maybe she wants him to stay by her side,*
*Maybe she wants to see how long it takes for him to*
*forget her voice,*
*how long will it take to forget that she was here, how*

*long till who she was..*

*Maybe she isn't lucky enough to take pride in herself and call him as her's...*

*How hard that would be to take the sacrifice at the cost of her feelings..*

*Her patience got tested with what her heart yearns the most..*

*Yelling she said - she herself will never be his poem beautifully written & composed,*

*She will never be a song remembered & sung,*

*She will never be a novel so coherent and captivating,*

*She will forever be the unwritten thought, the half finished story...*

*& a long forgotten melody, But..*

*she promised to keep him as her favourite incomplete story...*

*who would always be kept alive in her poetry...*

# 4. "Reminiscing Nature & You.."

*The fleeting breath of morning air, a soft voice that slips right through*
*No weight to hold, no time to bind, just moments shared with love in mind..*
*Make yourself feel through the whispers of the wind,*
*No matter how hard the battle gets in, there's nothing more glorious for the earth,*
*when someone refuses to give in to their most self hating, discouraged and delusional self,*
*& someone relishes the feeling of building a hut in the middle of the suffocating dust.*
*A brief respite of leisure & no rushing around*
*I want rainy days, lanterns & the moon twining in dark leaves,  some music spilling out & yet echoing inside my head...*
*All at once we were madly, clumsily, agonizingly in love;*
*hopelessly i should add, because that frenzy of mutual possession might have been assuaged,*
*Actually imbibing & assimilating every particle for each other's souls and flesh,*
*but there we failed to meet each other..*
*Thoughts rampaging my mind & bizzarely hitting my head*

*As if we were slum children that couldn't have the
opportunity to do so ..
there's vastness to grief that overwhelms ourselves
We are tiny, trembling clusters of atoms subsumed with
grief because of someone's awesome presence..
It occupies the core of our being & extends to the limits
of the universe..
As like love, grief is non negotiable, a terrible reminder
to measure the depth of love...
Grief & love are forever intertwined...
What I want is you see me, you look at your screen, you
say it'll pass, every word of mine will echo through the
ears..
Because it will, if you get to know me..
Right now I am a puzzle but not a mystery, But a work of
art.. word of literature...
If you get to know me you'll demystify the experience..
To take care of the wounds I wanted to talk about what
happened, without mentioning how much it hurt, there
has to be a way to name the pain...
Or so as to say --
I am honest with my pen, but not as much as when I
speak
If you ask me I would say everything is fine as it seems...
But when my eyes won't shut in the dead of the night,, i
pour ink on my paper and it writes:
Fading with the setting sun, making promises of truth,*

*If nothing lasts forever, could I be nothing to you?*
*Come! Meet me at the deadly nights where i shall*
*introduce myself to you...*
*Somewhere where the trees lull my body to sleep where*
*every promise is to be kept to stay alive which is meant*
*for you...*

# 5. "Unsaid Words.."

*In the quiet spaces, between each breath,*
*Where the heart beats its secret depth,*
*Lie the unsaid words, heavy and still,*
*Carried in silence, against their will.*
*They hover like shadows in the air,*
*A dance of thoughts, hidden with care.*
*They stayed in the corners of our mind,*
*Wishing to speak but always confined.*


*How many times have they longed to escape?*
*But the fear of truth reshapes their shape.*
*The unsaid words that never take flight,*
*And haunt us in the stillness of night.*
*They are the tears that never fall,*
*The longing that echoes, yet stays small.*
*The love that never found its voice,*
*The ache whispered, but had no choice.*


*At the softest glance, they find their way,*
*In the fleeting touch, in the words we don't say.*
*A heart is too afraid to break the glass,*
*Fearing the echoes of the moments that pass.*

And yet, they are imbibed within the chest,
A silent storm, a troubled guest.
These unsaid words are so full, so vast,
They are both a burden and a contrast.


For in the quiet, they often scream,
A reminder of the unspoken dream.
The dreams we dare not voice aloud,
Afraid they'll fade beneath the cloud.
In every glance we chose to hide,
In every step we took in pride,
The unsaid words weave through our veins,
A tangled web of joy and pains.


What is it that we fear to speak?
Is it rejection, or being weak?
Do we hold back to keep the peace,
To guard the love, to never cease?
Or is it shame that silences the soul,
The fear that our words will never be whole?
The unsaid words that flicker and fade,
As time runs by, their meaning is delayed.


Yet there are moments, fleeting and rare,

*When those unsaid words fill the air.*
*When courage blossoms, soft and true,*
*And we speak the words we never knew.*
*It's then we find the beauty, deep,*
*In the things we've hidden, buried, asleep.*
*The unsaid words that once held tight,*
*Become the stars that burn so bright.*
*And though we may never fully speak*
*Every thought that makes us weak,*
*Those unsaid words, in their own time,*
*Will find their rhythm, will find their rhyme.*
*They are the spaces between our song,*
*The echo that hums our whole life long.*
*The unsaid words, a silent art,*
*The heart's truth held close, never far.*

# 6. "My Beloved"

*You are the whisper in the breeze,*
*The calm that flows through the rustling trees.*
*In every moment, you are the softest sigh,*
*The twinkle of stars in the midnight sky.*
*You are the warmth in the coldest days,*
*The light that leads me through life's maze.*
*In your eyes, I find the world reborn,*
*A place where every sorrow is torn.*


*Your laughter is a melody so sweet,*
*A song that dances in every heartbeat.*
*In your presence, time moves slow,*
*As if the universe has let its glow.*
*Every word you speak is a sacred prayer,*
*You heal all the despair.*


*In you, I find my home,*
*A refuge from the world I've roamed.*
*With you, there's no need to pretend,*
*For in your heart, I find no end.*
*Your love is a river that endlessly flows,*
*Nourishing my spirit as it grows.*

*In every tear, every laugh, every sigh,*
*We build a world where hearts can fly.*


*You are the dream that never fades,*
*The promise in every gentle shade.*
*In your embrace, I feel the grace,*
*Of a love that time cannot erase.*
*Through every storm, through every fight,*
*You are my beacon, my guiding light.*
*Together, we conquer what life may bring,*
*For in your arms, I have everything.*


*My beloved, you are the moon in my night,*
*The sun that shines when the world feels right.*
*In the quiet of dawn, in the rush of day,*
*You are the reason I find my way.*
*In your love, I find my soul's release,*
*A perfect heaven, a place of peace.*
*Your love is a promise, forever true,*
*A bond that exists in all I do.*
*No words can capture the depth of you,*
*No song can sing what's pure and true.*
*For you are my heart, my life, my guide,*
*In you, I will forever reside.*
*Through every trial, through every grace,*

*I'll find you again in every place.*

*My love for you is vast,*

*The journey that will be forever first & forever last.*

# 7. "Seeing you through disguise"

*You wear a mask of sunlit grace,*
*A painted smile upon your face,*
*But in the stillness of your eyes,*
*I see the truth your heart denies.*
*The world may fall for practiced charm,*
*Entranced and blind to quiet harm,*
*But I have danced with shadowed light,*
*And know the soul that hides from sight.*

*Yet every note, though sweet and bright,*
*Carries a strain of silent fight.*
*Behind the smiles and painted eyes,*
*Lies the story masked by soft disguise.*
*I see through layers, thin and frail,*
*The silent cries, the hidden wail,*
*I reached out to touch, to lift the veil,*
*To find the soul hidden beneath the tale.*

*You speak in tones of certainty,*
*Of hopes and dreams and destiny—*
*But words can lie, and so can fate,*
*When built on fear I cultivate.*

*I've watched the way you turn away*
*From honest dawn to mimic day,*
*As if the truth would tear apart*
*You think I don't, but yes—I see*
*The ghost of who you used to be,*
*Before the world taught you to hide*
*The storms rage beneath the tide.*


*Each joke you tell,*
*Stabbed with a sharpened blade,*
*But I have learned the art of gaze,*
*And I see you through your maze.*
*The cracks are where the light pours in,*
*And I don't mind the flaws or sin.*
*Disguises fall, but I remain,*
*Unmoved by masks, unmoved by pain.*
*No perfect face could ever blind*
*The fierce soft fire I've come to find.*
*You wear your armor, play your role,*
*But I still see your inner soul.*


*And when the night is thick with lies,*
*I'll be the one who knows your skies.*
*So hide if you must—mask your cries—*
*But know: I see you through disguise.*

*And should you ever drop the veil,*
*I'll hold you close, still just as frail.*
*Not every truth needs grand reveal;*
*Sometimes it's enough to feel.*
*And feeling you, behind your eyes—*
*That's how I see through your disguise*

# 8. "Her love was a borrowed book"

*Pages whispering stories that were never mine.*
*Soft in my hands, with a fragrant past,*
*I held her gently, knowing it couldn't last.*
*Her laughter and ink, etched deep in my skin,*
*But the cover always closed before I could begin.*
*She came like a novel on someone's shelf,*
*Not quite for me, yet I lost myself.*
*In tales of a boy who once held her heart,*
*In chapters where I was never a part.*


*Her love wore dates, like a library stamp,*
*Moments borrowed beneath a flickering lamp.*
*Each word she had written with grace, with an*
*unfinished line,*
*The story was hers, but I made it mine.*
*I traced every sentence, reread each page,*
*Knew every silence, every quiet rage.*
*She was a romance with a tragic end,*
*The kind you return though you wish to pretend.*


*I longed to rewrite what was written before,*

*To keep her tucked in my soul.*
*But borrowed things must be set free,*
*No matter how deeply they dwell in thee.*
*One day, I turned the final sheet,*
*With trembling hands and reluctant feet.*
*Back to the shelf where all hearts go,*
*To rest between others who once let her go.*


*She smiled like endings that tasted bittersweet,*
*A tale incomplete yet hauntingly neat.*
*And though I only had a fleeting look,*
*I was a chapter in her borrowed book.*
*Now I walk with echoes of her love,*
*A reader once who wanted more.*
*But some love is not meant to be kept,*
*Only read, remembered, and quietly weep,*
*Her love was a borrowed book, I held it close,*
*But it was never mine to keep...*

# 9. "The last meeting..."

*In the quiet hush of the evening's glow,*
*Two hearts converge, then softly go.*
*Beneath the sky's melancholic hue,*
*They face the end they always knew.*


*The evening whispers secrets only they know,*
*As shadows encroach upon each heart.*
*Whispers between their last goodbyes.*
*Eyes that once sparkled with delight,*
*Now shattered with tears in fading light.*


*Fingers reach, then hesitate,*
*Bridging love and looming fate.*
*A touch that stayed, then retreats,*
*Echoing the rhythm of broken beats.*


*Memories flood the silent space,*
*Each one etched upon their face.*
*Laughter shared and dreams once spun,*
*Now shadows under the setting sun.*

*The world around them fades away,*
*As sorrow paints the close of day.*
*Words unspoken hang in the air,*
*A testament to the love they bear.*


*A single tear trails down her cheek,*
*He longs to speak but can't yet speak.*
*The weight of parting, heavy and deep,*
*Promises made, now hard to keep.*


*Silent words in the space where love resigns,*
*With trembling lips, the truths they cannot speak.*
*Then turning slowly, paths divide,*
*Two souls drift on sorrow's tide.*


*Yet in the chambers of their minds,*
*The other's presence intertwined.*
*Though separate journeys they embark,*
*Their last meeting ignites the dark.*


*For love once kindled never dies,*
*It stayed under the distant skies.*

*And though they are apart, their spirits stay,*
*Forever touched, come what may.*

# 10. "Echoes of a Fading heart"

*In twilight,  where silence sighs,*
*A heartbeat wanes, beneath the skies.*
*Once vibrant chords of passion's song,*
*Now drift as echoes, faint and long.*


*The laughter shared, the tender grace,*
*Now shadows dance in empty space.*
*Each memory, a whispered plea,*
*A ghost of what we used to be.*


*The touch that sparked a fervent fire,*
*Now cold as ash, devoid of desire.*
*Eyes that once held stars alight,*
*Now mirror voids of endless night.*


*Promises etched in time's embrace,*
*Now scattered leaves, lost in space.*
*The warmth that wrapped our souls as one,*
*Now faded with the setting sun.*

*Yet in this void, a subtle sound,*
*A distant echo, softly bound.*
*A trace of love that once was near,*
*Still lingers in the atmosphere.*


*Though hearts may fade and dreams depart,*
*The echoes dwell within the heart.*
*A testament to love's refrain,*
*A melody of joy and pain.*


*So let these echoes gently guide,*
*Through corridors where memories hide.*
*For even as the heartbeats part,*
*Love's echo sings within the heart.*

# 11. "Talked with the night sky"

*When I talked about his eyes,*
*I wasn't talking only about the colour of his lenses he*
*has;*
*But the sparkle was as if they were celestial.. When I*
*talked about his smile, it was as if the*
*moon brightened all of the dark nights..*
*Nights where I smiled staring at him...*
*His name was mentioned in the rooms of my heart he*
*hadn't visited,*
*his majestic words echoed my ear...*

*He had been the brightest star of my Galaxy,*
*yet I would like to be the falling star who would*
*disappear from the sky,,*
*Like the Andromeda never meets the Milky way!*
*Distance apart from the moon, i would say from far...*
*For stars of heaven and their constellations won't give*
*their light;*
*The sun would be darker at the time of rising, but the*
*moon would never shed its light...*

*At times her heart screams to the divine, for she, being*
*cruel to herself...*

To keep him as a secret of her life, she tried hard not to
unfold things she wanted to..
At times she writes to hold her emotions inside, But how
could even she forget that
it wasn't even a single night, had she not searched for
her moon,
Her grief no one else, only her pillow could give the
proof...
To keep him like an oath she disappeared in the vastness
of the sky...
Both run in the parallel universe, the falling star seems
to fade her light but she still hopes her moon shines
bright...

# 12. "Untold words..."

*So much untold*
*It's a story of a heart, nowhere to unfold.*
*Briefly becoming eternal Words of a dead journal, Her*
*life isn't normal, May be it's accidental..*

*No destiny or fate*
*Knew that the truth was late.*
*She was voided at the end!*
*She loved, she cared, she fought*
*She was selfless..*


*Most of her unhappiness was self inflicted as if to the*
*pain she was addicted; And slowly she died With the*
*regrets that made her cry Because she knew-*
*Her heart wasn't a lie...*


*World of memories dipped in which is yet unvisited &*
*untold With a love so hellbent, massacred at the hands of*
*feelings & time.*
*She sang her song of love, song of pain,*
*Pure as a dove her soul touched with drops of rain*
*She hidden her heart with her words of cheers, Beyond*

*her smile were truthful tears,*


*Forbidden in her mouth or in her heart this time:*
*She cried a little longer, hurted a little stronger..*
*Today with all the grief inside she acted like*
*she is a drunkard,*
*But this time uncontrollably she penned down*
*everything on a piece of paper...*

# 13. "Her balcony"

*Choked by the conversation stuck in my throat; Waiting
in desperation for me to find the words, Words hiding
under my tongue;*
*Now escaping me when I see her around..*
*The confession itching my insides!*
*But I am terrified of how they'll sound to her when they
come unstuck...*

*Her balcony doesn't judge her, as often it is -*
*A place so tiny where she stands to differentiate between
Choice & Destiny,*
*A place beyond every definition of every Thought &
Imagination,*
*A place beyond every Questions & Answers, where she
had poured down all her tears!*
*A place which has seen many wounds of her heart that
have never bleeded!!*

*Shackled with every emotion; thinking herself as a
Scarlet of a floral stage,*
*She has found her changed body, her withered soul,
broken pieces of her heart & stressed mind!*
*Wounds are not healed with time...*

*It only reminded her how she has fought through her mind,*
*And taught her that she has never played blind!*


*"She was a miserly sold out concert of true heart*
*Slowly & slowly turning herself into a cold stoneheart..."*
*She used to love the ocean until she drowned; Where her*
*pain hinted like a drop in its vastness..*


*When the world was sleeping, she walked*
*around the silent streets...*
*Whispering in symphony-*
*"At every dawn & dusk she witnessed on her balcony,*
*Immersed in Mystery, she spelled out everything in her*
*Poetry..."*

# 14. "HE...."

*Although I saw someone in black scrub holding a
stethoscope;
A person whom I didn't know
In these unknown streets, out of nowhere,
He was the strangest circumstance that had happened in
life.
I slowly walked into his life & got it right where
everyone else got it wrong..
A man whose personality was 'in a Galore'
His smile depicts the truth He had in him..
His straightforward nature showed how benevolent he
is!
His charm attracted many eyes, but nature attracted
mine..
A man who is uncared for, who smiled at any situation,
He, with his many personified characters trespassed my
life,
His nature compelled me & my curiosity to know him
more..
He holds his secrets close to his chest,
A keeper of silence, a man of unrest.
He speaks with actions, not with his voice,
His savage reply, his humour, everything became my
choice..*

*Naughty He, fitness freak He, photographer He, Topic*
*He, but now the writer is me..*
*Every part of him, He beholds*
*started to make me smile;*
*even though I felt shy to come in front of him*
*I talked & manifested many memories with his car which*
*I've always searched for...*
*Now I can't find words, the human part in me said-*
*I've always knocked on his door, I felt like home..*
*As I am feeling dormant in his absence:*
*my tears broke the silence, saying*
*I'm fine would be the biggest lie to me!*
*It was an instant recognition, a passionate connection,*
*something other-worldly,*
*Painful though parting be; I bow down & owe everything*
*to him,*
*He etched an irreplaceable space in my heart forever,*
*Gave many reasons to laugh, love him, a true man to*
*admire!!*
*Showering lots of love & respect, from the bottom of my*
*heart I would say,*
*Looking at you I became a poet without a pen,*
*Your soul is vast, yet tightly held,*
*A world of wonders, silently dwelled.*
*You are the listener when I need to speak,*
*The shelter I seek when the world feels weak.*
*You are the rock in an endless sea,*

*The hand I reach for when you can't see.*
*You are, simply, the man who understands,*
*You are the silence that speaks so clear,*
*A mystery unfolding, about you there's so much more,*
*A universe of wisdom, forever to explore...*

# 15. "A birthday wish..."

*Not a year goes by without this day*
*While happiness is sought in every way*
*but know that the love you get today,*
*will stay forever & all the way...;*


*With every year, you're more divine,*
*Forever young at heart, the man so fine...*
*You're known & always respected for your*
*'Nature which is 'An utterly Bliss....'*


*And so to honour this, you can take hold of a Gift.*
*A mind that I can comprehend and be blessed to believe,*
*Knowing someone as fabulous as me should be the only*
*present you need...*


*To an Isle full of joy, laughter is the only image.*
*on your face, sheer vibrance in your eyes..*
*Adored is the heart, for kindness, that has shaped*
*Redeemed is the soul, blessed are the one that beholds!!*

*The man whose personality is 'in a Galore'*
*A guide, a true man to be admired!*
*If I had been fortunate enough to have a friend in You, I*
*would treasure the time always...*


*So on your day, my never-ending serenade, Sending you*
*with all the Harmonious voice of the Nightingales, the*
*Moon, the Sea-Waves*
*& Mine of course...*
*With all the love of gratitude, To my Hunky Dory...*
*"Wishing you a very Happy Birthday for all the years..."*

# 16. "You... My favourite topic"

*And when I kept you in the verse of my poetry,*
*I didn't know your name shall echo in every page I turn...*
*Over the chapters I intend to fill, blended with each word*
*that dared to find a space...*
*Being the writer, you were always my words..*
*Sunsets, night sky, moonlight walks, everything always*
*conspires me to bring me back to you!*
*So I have created my own canvases that drape my heart,*
*Each carrying a wish that I whisper every night...*
*Many unwritten confessions are stuck in my throat,*
*Neither I could speak nor can I assimilate...*
*So seeing myself in the mirror, I trusted it and wanted to*
*confess everything to it suddenly I remember -*
*Words do not express thoughts very well,*
*They always become a little different immediately when*
*they are expressed, sounding a little distorted, a little*
*foolish.. So I kept myself mute!*
*So internalizing my chaos instead, I would say-*
*The first time I met you was the last time I wasn't*
*thinking about you..*
*Some of the happiest places are in my mind with you;*
*I don't need to see the world, but I can't stop myself from*
*feeling you..*

*You feel so familiar to me that I must have loved you in more than one lifetime!*

*You are a never ending thought...*

*A charming gardener that has bloomed me in the Bounty of Paradise!!*

*Sometimes you just can't explain what you see in a person,*

*It just takes you to a place where no one else can...*

*Distance tried to come between us & so did life but were always connected ..*

*Sometimes with words, sometimes with silence, sometimes with souls... Nothing could stop it not even the time itself!!*

*To sit day & night, to contemplate the image of my beloved, the heart seeks those moments...*

*Often I go silent whenever I see you happy pulling my legs, being kiddish to me;*

*I do smile from my end!*

*Always have a hope to listen a line from you..*

*But falling apart,, even if you ask the moon it will always smile at you & say - "All Hail you Prince..!"*

*Once again the fresh display of charm catches the eyes..*

*I feel part of my soul loves you so much, maybe we are from the same star...*

*Connected to you with an intangible thread which may stretch but it will never break..*

*Still the eyes will tell you more than words could ever*

*say ; or so as to say -*

*You are my believer, beloved & a caretaker of all my*

*secrets!!*

# 17. "IF..."

*I don't know the literature of describing what love is..*
*I only know- it is the emotion which beholds kindness,*
*generosity, and respect.*
*If seeing you bring a smile to my face,*
*If seeing you at the top of the world makes me happy,*
*If your touch makes me feel differently,*
*If my jealousy is there to share with others,*
*If my soul has started sensing you,*
*If my happiness exists staring at you,*
*If loving you deeply gives me courage,*
*If you are the last thought that comes to my mind when I*
*am drifted off to my sleep.*
*In spite of your imperfection, if I have fallen for You,*
*If your beliefs have made me believe that you are there*
*for me.*
*If seeing you weak,  unhappy has put me in pain,*
*If seeing you cry, someday will make me teary..*
*If your heart is meant to be in love with you,*
*If my eyes have always seen the best in you,*
*If I behave childishly, it provides happiness to me*
*irritating you,*
*If your conversations have always encouraged me*
*If your touch has melted me down.*
*If your eyes have always spoken the truth to me,*

*If your faith in me, has restricted me to many undone*
*If your words played a beautiful melody in my ears while*
*I fell asleep...*
*If someday I expect to be loved by you,*
*If someday your weird nature has affected me,*
*If someday I start missing you more,*
*If someday hugging you, listening to your increased*
*heartbeat has provided me the place, I wanted !*
*If someday I felt something like home somehow...*
*If someday I sworn onto keep you like an oath*
*In the middle of the night today, running scared ;*
*I will say it's love, but you wondered what it was !!*
*So maybe I lost my translation,*
*Maybe I asked for too much,*
*Maybe I am not good at telling you jokes, but,*
*The punchline goes - I still remember it all, how it*
*happened...*
*If only these, a few limiting lines have defined what love*
*Is ?? Then -*
*Yeah, it is love, I am in love with true obedience,*
*voluntarily, not compelled by fear or any force, without*
*any expectation from my beloved!*

# 18. "The distance between us.."

*The distance between us is not just a line*
*It's a distance of a couple of days far*
*Drawn on maps, or measured in time.*
*Yet we both are different, the parallel lines,*
*Traveling side by side, through miles..*


*It is the hush between two heartbeats slow,*
*The silence where our whispers used to go.*
*It is the ache that shadows the moon,*
*The essence of you that fades too soon.*
*A cold pillow, an echoing room,*
*Where once bloomed laughter, now lies gloom.*


*I reach for you in the quiet of night,*
*Where dreams blur wrong and right.*
*Your name, a song upon my lips,*
*Still dances in each breath I sip.*


*I count the stars like promises made,*
*Wishing they'd bring you near me to stay.*

*Each one is a memory, soft and kind,*
*That harboured gently in my mind.*


*The distance, you can't afford*
*In stories left half-said, untold.*
*In the morning light you do not see,*
*And sunsets that don't wait for me.*


*Yet, love, though miles may stretch so wide,*
*It flows like tides we cannot hide.*
*Across the fields of space and doubt,*
*It speaks in ways that silence shouts.*


*You stole my heart like a charming game,*
*Now it warms me when I call your name.*
*Your voice— I want to listen as a whole,*
*That binds & enlightens my soul.*


*This distance is very cruel,*
*But cannot steal what means so much.*
*For hearts like ours know how to wait,*
*How to bend but not break under fate.*

*Each day apart, a step toward you,*
*Each tear I cry, a love made true.*
*And though you're far, you're always near,*
*In every thought, in every tear.*


*I close my eyes, and you are there,*
*Your smile lifts my ear,*
*Eagerly waiting year after year..*
*Your laughter is the best,*
*Where even time dares not to rest.*


*The distance may stretch wide and vast,*
*But this love was built to last.*
*And when the miles melt into one,*
*Hope to rise again as one.. .*


*So hold on, love, and wait for me,*
*Beyond the land, beyond the sea.*
*For love like ours, no roads are too long—*
*You are the lyrics of my favourite song.*

# 19. "Is Writing Supposed to Heal?"

*Is writing supposed to heal —*
*this trembling hand,*
*I trace the paper's empty field,*
*and ask if ink can mend what bleeds.*
*I press my sorrows into lines,*
*and find the blood sips through the rhyme.*
*They told me stories mend the heart,*
*that metaphors can break apart*
*They say a word can lift a stone,*
*can find the broken, bring them home;*
*that every letter stitched in pain*
*can seam together scattered names.*


*But what of scars are too deep for sound,*
*what of the silence that resounds?*
*I spill my ink, I tear the air,*
*but grief just sits, an unwashed prayer.*
*I write and write — the aching stays,*
*like a ghost that will not turn away.*
*I built a house of sentences,*
*but storms still tear right through the ribs.*
*Each sentence is built, each verse unfurled,*

*a paper shield against the world.*


*I write — not healed, but slightly seen,*
*A wound named is not a wound undone;*
*it only learns to face the sun.*
*Perhaps it's not to heal at all,*
*but to remember how we fall.*
*Perhaps the act of reaching out,*
*is braver than the healing found.*


*To shape the hurt, to give it a voice,*
*to honor even the shattered noise —*
*to sit with sorrow, hand in hand,*
*and say: I do not understand,*
*So maybe writing's not the cure,*
*but proof that's still I can endure —*
*that in the ash of what won't mend,*
*I carve a shape, I call it Friend.*
*And maybe that's the secret art:*
*not healing, but a kind of start —*
*a slow becoming, word by word,*
*a way to bear what can't be cured...*

# 20. "And How It Started..."

*I believe poetry happens to a poet long way before they
ever write it...*
*I always love to sit in melancholy and think of nature
and quote lines –*
*With deadly words, no feelings, no emotions within.*
*Then, there comes a person in my life,*
*Somehow, he made me pick up a pen;*
*Suddenly, turning my silence into words.*
*Words that were deadly, started to take hold of feelings !*
*I started to decipher my own emotions into words.*
*I started to get closer and find meanings amongst natural
things.*
*Sitting beneath the trees with the moonlight in the
streets, the stars, the twilight,*
*Started whispering his name;*
*Deep down in the core of my heart, started believing his
fame;*
*Quietly in my eardrums, the wave hitting the seashore
started playing the game with his name.*
*Elated with the fact, the angels in his form have started
to walk beside me,*
*Provided me the protection, support on the journey, I
have chosen to walk.*
*There's no limit to the way he entered into my life and*

*won it.*
*Both of us walk on different roads ,*
*I pondered, how can I become so true?*
*Separated paths , I asked God –*
*Should I end the story? God replied, –*
*Nah! Continue till destiny!*
*I then finally realised, I found my rhythm in you,*
*Steps that were taken backwards, thrown me closer to*
*you.*
*Even I wonder, all those I compose, I paint, manage to*
*escape –*
*the madness, melancholia, the pain, and the fear*
*which was inherent in me,*
*started vanishing because of you.*
*Life is like a song, where your voice is my tune*
*Life is like poetry, where your words are my composition*
*Life is like a picture, where your smile keeps me alive.*
*Everything around me, makes sense, whenever there is*
*you,*
*Everything around me, seems promising when standing*
*tall with you.*
*I always had a wish that every time you sense me,*
*I want you to take me as your responsibility,*
*In every turn of my life, make a promise to just stay...*
*As with you, I seem to be perfect, anyway ...*

# 21. "The Promise I Kept..."

*I once gave you a promise, quiet yet strong,*
*Carried in whispers, in silence, in song.*
*Through nights that were endless, through doubt and*
*through fear,*
*I stitched every word with you holding me near.*
*When the pages grew heavy, and silence had crept,*
*I leaned on the vow—the promise I kept.*
*To weave you a story, to give you my best.*


*You asked not for riches, nor castles in skies,*
*Just pages and ink, spun with truth, spun with lies.*
*A book with your name etched deep in its bones,*
*A shelter of words, a kingdom, million of tones.*


*I held it so tightly, this oath, this thread,*
*Through sleepless mornings and nights filled with dread.*
*When doubt's heavy fingers , revolved around my pen,*
*I'd remember your smile—and begin once again.*


*Each chapter a footstep, each sentence a sigh,*
*Each character breathing the dreams I let fly.*

*Your faith was my compass, your hope was my light,*
*Guiding my hand through the valleys of night.*
*Each line holds a heartbeat, each chapter a sigh,*
*Each word is a wing, teaching sorrow to fly.*
*You trusted my hands with a world yet unwept,*
*And today, here it stands—the promise I kept.*


*I wrote about the battles I fought in my mind,*
*Of the scars and the triumphs I gather through time.*
*I wrote of a friendship the stars would applaud,*
*Of promises whispered and witnessed by God.*
*The ink still smells fresh, the pages still sing,*
*Of oceans and cities and flight without wings.*


*Here is your story, your laughter, your tears,*
*A book stitched together from pieces of years.*
*Here is the promise, once trembling and new—*
*A tapestry whole, made for no one but you.*
*I kept it, my dear, through the storm and the test,*
*I honored the vow beating loud in my chest.*


*And as you now hold it, and smile or you weep,*
*Know this is the promise I fought for—and keep.*
*Know this is a story spun all from me for you.*

*Take it, my friend, it was born as you slept—*
*A song made of ink,*

*And 'The promise I kept....'*

9 789370 927902